TRAINING POINTERS AND SETTERS

Training Pointers and Setters

J. B. Maurice

South Brunswick and New York:
A. S. Barnes and Company

© Dr J. B. Maurice 1974

First American edition published 1975 by
A. S. Barnes and Company, Inc., Cranbury, New Jersey 08512

Library of Congress Catalog Card Number: 74-17763

ISBN 0-498-01678-1

Printed in the United States of America

Contents

Contents

Illustrations

7

ILLUSTRATIONS

IN TEXT

Glossary

This should be read carefully as the terms used have an exact meaning, often not quite what might be expected.

Backing   stopping on seeing another dog pointing

Beat   the area and/or the method of hunting

Blinking   coming away from a point as the handler approaches

Bore into wind   hunt straight or too straight into the wind

Cast   the direction in which a dog is sent or hunts

Down wind   following the wind direction when the wind blows the scent away from the dog

Flushing   making the birds fly either at command or by stopping too late

Gun   the man hoping to shoot, not necessarily the handler

Handler   in the literal sense, the person who pats,

combs, feeds and leads; and who also directs the
work of the dog in the field

Haunt   the place from which the birds have flown

Larking   hunting small birds and not attending to
business

Nose   the ability to find birds—not entirely sense of
smell, partly bird-finding brains

Pointing   to become stationary in a characteristic
attitude on locating game; also known as setting

Roading   following the track of already pointed
birds

Running in   chasing birds when shot or flushed

Setting   see *Pointing*

Stickiness   not moving freely in to flush birds after
pointing

Touch   faint smell of birds

Up wind   the direction from which the wind is
blowing

Wild birds   birds difficult to approach

THE HANDLER'S PRAYER

Send me the guns safe, silent and swift,
Send me a beat that's in the wind's drift,
Send me a fair and unwavering breeze,
Send me the dogs who will steadily freeze,
Send me the guns who can shoot on the wing,
Send me retrievers kept on the string,
Send me the dogs who the whistle will heed,
Send me occasional coveys at need,
Send me a wife who does not complain,
   when soaked to the skin by hail or rain,
Send me a host who's been dogging before,
Send me and my team safely home from the moor.

J.B.M.

Acknowledgement

The basic principles of this method of training appeared in General Hutchinson's book *Dog Breaking*, which I first read in 1940. Times have changed since he wrote it in 1848, but I am greatly indebted to his ideas. Following the written word, I trained my first dog to field trial standard although I had never seen a pointer or setter in action before.

Introduction

The use of dogs to locate game birds without flushing them is an ancient craft. It is a craft which can be learned from a book. A handler can be of either sex, requiring no great strength or experience. All that he or she needs is patient perseverence and the ability to walk. Being a good shot, or even being able to shoot at all, is unnecessary. In fact, a handler who does not shoot is always popular with the organiser of a shoot.

ANCESTRY OF THE POINTING DOGS

The first dogs used in England were called spaniels. I believe there is in existence a thirteenth-century legal document recording a contract to teach a spaniel to 'sett'. These spaniels developed into the modern setter. The earliest use of the pointing dogs was for netting game and, to a lesser extent, to aid the hawks. The coveys were netted by two men dragging a net over the crouching dog, which accounts for the tendency of present-day setters to crouch when pointing.

Pointers seem to have been brought into England about 1713 by soldiers returning home after the Peace of Utrecht. Probably of Spanish origin, they were called 'puntas' after the Spanish word 'to point'. They were well established by 1725, as is shown by a painting of the Duke of Kingston with a brace of the breed. All pointers and setters were working dogs at one time. *The Art of Shooting Flying* appeared in 1767, when shooting over dogs must already have been popular.

In his book *The Setter*, published in 1872, Edward Laverack wrote: 'Many years before *The Field* was in existence or dog shows or field trials thought of, my breed of setters had made their mark . . . I purpose to give a short but faithfull description of the different varieties I know of.' At seventy-three years of age, Laverack had more than fifty years' experience of breeding. He lists the strains of setters in this order:

1 The Earl of Carlisle, Naworth Castle, Brampton, Cumberland.
    Liver and white
2 Lord Lovat, Beaufort Castle, Beauly, Inverness-shire.
    Black, white and tan
3 The Earl of Southesk, Forfarshire.
    Black, white and tan
4 The Earl of Seafield, Urquhart Castle, Inverness-shire.

Black, white and tan. Lemon or orange and
white
5 Lord Ossulston, Chillingham Castle, Wooler,
Northumberland.
Black
6 Mr Lort, Kings Norton, Birmingham.
Black and white. Lemon and white
7 The Llanidloes, Welsh Setters.
Milk or chalk white
8 The Russian Setter. (I think Laverack saw
only one specimen.)
White. Lemon and white. Liver and white.
Black and white
9 The Gordon Setter, or Black and Tan Setter.
Black and tan
Laverack states that the Duke of Gordon
liked black, white and tan colouring as it was
gayer and not so difficult to back on the hill.
The composite colour was produced by using
black-and-tan dogs to black-and-white
bitches. In July 1836 eleven of these setters
averaged 36 guineas each; that is, more than
the *annual* wage of the game keeper, who then
earned about 10s a week.
10 English Setters. (Laverack's own breed.)
Black greys. Blue or lemon and white
Belton—fleabitten or with small close flecks
11 Irish Setter.
Blood red with a black shade at the tips of
the coat. Others blood red and white. Both
are stated to have a proportion of black pups

It would seem that in Laverack's time there were many colours to choose from. Sadly, with the exception of the Irish Setter, the whole colours have gone. Now the English Setters can be classed as tricolour black and occasional tan ticks on white; lemon or orange and white. I have never seen a black-and-white working English Setter with no tan at all.

Laverack also says in his book: 'Driving and not using dogs has caused the habits of the game to change and also more shooters, less cover and a greater population, but worse still inattentive breeding is spoiling dogs.' This comment has a very modern sound: I first heard it said in 1914 and it has been repeated almost every year since. In the early 1800s the quantity of birds and the superlativeness of the dogs must have been breathtaking! On the other hand, two of today's oldest living handlers—both close on ninety years old and among the finest in their profession—have praised present-day dogs on two occasions as being the best they had ever seen. One of these men claimed to have handled at sixteen and the other to have led dogs at eight, at field trials.

Edward Laverack's strain passed on to a Mr Llewellin, who ran and imported setters extensively to the USA and Europe. His strain is separately registered in the USA but nowhere else. The terms Llewellin, Laverack and Belton are still used in Europe to indicate descent from Laverack's original dogs.

Page 17 (*left*) Contact between dog and handler forges a bond between them and helps concentration; (*right*) Eyes on the face, a sure sign that partnership has been established and confidence is complete

Page 18 (*above*) The trainer's kit. On his van are leather gloves, whistles, short check cord on the left, slip lead, and long check cord on reel; (*below*) First lessons indoors. The 'To Ho' being taught to a puppy in an empty barn

THE WORKING BREEDS

Since dog shows became fashionable, the working breeds have been widely shown. A separation developed between the show and working strains, and argument between the breeders of the two strains became heated. This separation is more marked in some breeds than others. The qualities of conformation and temperament are judged under very different circumstances in the show ring and in the shooting field.

Recent scientific facts about dog breeding are given in a most informative and interesting book, *Inheritance in Dogs with Special Reference in the Hunting Breeds* by the Danish geneticist, Ojvinde Winge. Dogs have seventy-eight chromosomes, of which thirty-nine come from each parent. The chromosomes can be combined in any order—the thirty-ninth with the first, second or third, for example—and the number of possible variations is enormous. Certain factors, such as colour, size and shape of ears, can be determined in advance of the mating. Winge states, however, that the inheritance of mental characteristics is far more difficult to explain. These cannot be expressed in a few words and cannot be measured; as a rule it is a question of degree. Therefore, the breeding of dogs for work seems to consist of selecting proved workers and crossing them in a common-sense manner, assessing the result of the experiment by the performance of the progeny.

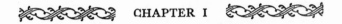 

CHAPTER I

The End in View

Before a handler undertakes the training of a pointing dog, it is essential to grasp what are the objects to be attained.

THE SENSE OF SMELL

Dogs have the power of locating things by smell—a power which man does not experience to the same degree. The sensation of smell is caused by particles in the air which stimulates the olfactory nerves. It can be visualised as steam or smoke moving down wind and gradually becoming dissipated until undetectable. The main source seems to be the oil on skin, fur or feathers. A fingerprint smells and certainly the same deposit from the pheasant's foot is detectable to a dog. The scent comes either from the creature directly or from objects coated with the oily deposit.

I had a partially blind and deaf setter who could hunt brilliantly in old age. He never responded to the whistle or hand signal, but could locate me in a mass of people by scent at distances up to about 200 yds —returning that distance between the posts on the racehorse training gallop when he had lost me. He would only do this up wind. It was necessary to position myself so that the wind blew towards him. I was not flattered by his ability! This power would be magical in man. What his world was like in youth when his senses were more acute is difficult to imagine. Into this world your puppy is born and will be trained.

HOW DOGS WORK

Hunting dogs can be divided into three classes: the tracking dogs—hounds and retrievers—which follow the footsteps; flushing dogs, which flush the game, locating it either by following the foot scent or finding the body scent; and locating dogs, which should locate the game by body scent alone.

I do not mean that tracking and flushing dogs take off after every line they cross. Trained and experienced animals are clever and selective in their hunting. Fox hounds stick to the fox, disregarding deer and hares; retrievers follow the wounded and find the dead, disregarding the others. Spaniels learn to find and move their game with skill and judgement.

I am stressing the difference between the types of work. Tracking dogs should work following the line with their noses close to the ground, while locating dogs should keep their heads high to catch the airborne body scent. Locating dogs should find the game rather than the place it has recently left. I believe that clever locating dogs know from faint foot scent that game is in the area, but work to locate it by body scent.

THE DOG'S BEAT

Think of it diagrammatically. Crossing the wind direction, the sense of smell covers, say, 25 yards by the length of the dog's cast, say, 100 yards. If his next cast is correctly done, he advances 25 yards and covers with his nose another 2,500 square yards and misses nothing.

Cheek wind

People talk rather loosely of a 'cheek wind'. This term should mean a wind coming from 45° right or left of the handler's path of advance. Hunting a cheek wind, the dog is not crossing at right angles to the handler's line of advance. The following diagrams will help to show this:

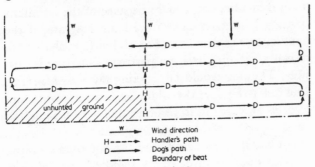

W→	Wind direction
H ---→	Handler's path
D ——→	Dog's path
—·—·—	Boundary of beat

THE END IN VIEW

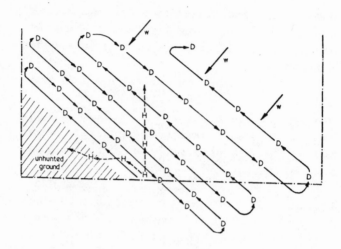

The dog is in front of the handler on the left and behind on the right—or the other way with a different wind direction. The dog's beat is about one-sixth longer on a cheek wind or the width of the area is reduced by one-sixth. The ground is made good perfectly satisfactorily. For inexperienced dogs, it is more difficult than it looks because of the handler's position behind or in front. In the diagram, if the handler moves down wind to his left (handler's path shown at bottom left), no pattern of hunting is possible. The dog would be working away to his right. The faster the dog, the wider his beat, allowing him to cross 25 yards in front of his handler on each half cast.

If the gun does 2 mph and the dog does 20 mph, the dog does 10 yards to the handler's 1 yard. The dog goes out to the left $112\frac{1}{2}$ yards, advances 25 yards into the wind and turns $112\frac{1}{2}$ yards; while the handler does 25 yards and repeats the process on the right.

The handler stands still for the first half cast. Although 225 yards does not sound very far, it covers about the same front as five guns walking 45 yards apart. A man working his dog gets five times as many chances as the walking gun and is alert and ready for them all!

This is only approximate, but it shows the need for a regular beat so that ground is not missed and the dog can be watched. If a dog with a regular beat vanishes, you can expect to find him where he disappeared. You may think both man and dog slow, but heather and hills reduce speed.

THE DOG ON POINT

When the dog locates game, he indicates its presence the instant he is aware of it and remains stationary on point until asked to advance or he drops automatically to wing. Pointing should override dropping to wing and shot, if the dog knows more game is present. He stays on point or should do so. Do not ask him to retrieve, he deserves a rest after the shots.

All these manoeuvres should be conducted in silence. Even the guns should not talk! Each point is a hunt on its own, and all the guns in the party should be in on it.

Differences in pointing style

The idiosyncracies of the pointing breeds are not constant and vary very much with each dog.

Pointers usually stand up boldly on point and road forward steadily and quietly. Some are very hard-headed about ground treatment, often getting very close to their birds for this reason.

English Setters are the most prone to set or sit on point, to be sticky in starting to road and going in short rushes. This last makes for quick roading and gets birds up well. It needs to be controlled by the signal or word of command to stop still. Often English Setters can learn to beat the ground to perfection. Some strains are natural backers.

Gordon Setters are inclined to be very hard galloping dogs and to creep forward after pointing, which can be disastrous. Their pointing is usually most decisive.

Irish Setters have a tendency to feather—that is, stop and wag their tails—instead of pointing stiffly. This makes their points rather indecisive for the handler who may be unable to help his puppy as quickly as he should. Like the Gordon Setter, the Irish Setter tends to revel in galloping and not to hunt with caution.

All the breeds can work to perfection, but the picture varies quite a lot and must be allowed for in training. Bitches are always more forward than their brothers, often working as if they were two or three months older.

CHAPTER 2

Early Days

A POINTING DOG'S PEDIGREE

A puppy from parents of proven working ability is the most likely to respond to training. Dogs have been selected for their skill and tractability in pointing game for a very long time; some pedigrees can be traced to 1840 or before. It seems foolish to throw away the advantages of that long selection for any consideration. The maternal line is the most important. People breed from famous and fashionable sires, which are almost invariably good workers, but seem inclined to overlook the bitches' capabilities or lack of them. In-bred dogs may have undesirable defects which often take years to show. In-breeding and line-breeding are difficult to define. In-breeding might be said to consist of first cousin or nearer matings for three generations. Line-breeding might be defined as rejoining the same strain after three or four generations.

The pedigree below illustrates this point.

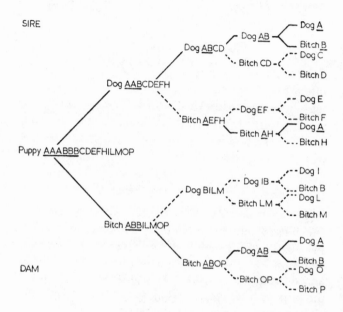

This is breeding back to the strain AB which was the admired dog. As there is about a one-third chance of great similarity, I would consider this pedigree as line-breeding and quite safe. Putting in AB twice more would be in-breeding.

In-breeding may be necessary and desirable if unsatisfactory animals are culled ruthlessly and eliminated. It is a very tricky business. Factors may be recessive and not show until a combination of them eliminates the dominant factor. In English Setters black colour is dominant, red a recessive, which is why occasionally a red puppy is born to black parents.

CHOOSING A PUPPY

Selecting a young puppy is a gamble. The smallest is often the sharpest, while the biggest has had the least pressure to use his brains. The qualities that matter most are those of the special senses—hearing, smelling and seeing—and the intelligence to use them. The body only acts as a vehicle for these qualities; though a poor body will, of course, mean early fatigue and a dulling of the mind and nerves. Choose the puppy that attracts you, but go for moderation in all things—in size, shape and temperament. The question of temperament is a difficult factor: a bold pup may be indifferent to his handler and a timid one too nervous to correct. Try to leave the pup with his mother until he is twelve weeks old. This seems to make them do better.

Colour

Boldly marked dogs are easier to see on the heather than whole-coloured ones or those marked with dense small flecks. Most young puppies become more heavily marked with age. You may think that invisibility would help to prevent the dog scaring his quarry. I do not think this is so; his breathing and the noise of his progress are quite loud enough to alert the birds. When he stops, the birds watch him and the bold colouring may hold their attention. Shepherds talk of a dog having 'an eye', meaning that the sheep stay quiet when he stands and watches them. I have noticed in sheep-dog trials that those who have this quality are often strikingly marked about the head.

DOMESTICATION

Having selected your pup, when you take him home, domesticate him. By this I mean that he needs to be handled, brushed, combed, carried, led about and hand-fed. If at all possible, have him indoors at times, also in the car and with people. It is often said that members of the family in the house ruin a gun dog, which should be kept in the kennel. I agree that a kennel, with a pen in which he can be shut, is essential to prevent wandering and self-hunting, and also for his own safety. It is true that commands must be obeyed and that it is impossible, for instance, to enforce obedience and carry on a telephone conversation at the same time; but half an hour by the fire or in the sitting-room has a huge educational value for the puppy and forges a link between him and the handler. It is a case of being sensible and only having the animal indoors when a reasonable amount of attention can be given him.

The kennel should be kept warm, dry and clean, with the pen of sufficient size to allow exercise. A kennel of, say, 6 feet by 4 feet is ideal for up to three dogs. A pen of the same size means that no exercise can be taken, but with a run of 20 yards in length, the dogs can dash about. Bigger runs may be better, but in half an acre puppies will gallop themselves to skin and bone.

Give the pup freedom to run about in suitable places; call his name and get him to come to you with pleasure for a pat and praise. Try and let him be clean away from his kennel and the house. It is natural for dogs to be clean, and puppyhood lasts only a very short time.

Get him accustomed to wearing a collar and lead. Be very gentle and make him come along without dragging him. Do not try to teach him to walk to heel until he is happy pulling on the lead.

The ideal routine with a very young puppy would be to put him on his lead, take him to a nearby paddock and let him have a race round, calling him back and making much of him. Give him a longer walk later in the day. Feed him and have him in the house for an hour then put him to bed. The routine should be changed for an older dog and, with the puppy's development, exercise should be increased.

DIET

Puppies

A pup's diet must contain some milk, some flesh, some cod liver oil and some starch. Bones are a pleasure and good for his teeth, but not essential regularly if he has milk. Brown bread, brown sugar and milk with a teaspoonful of cod liver oil, if associated with a little red meat, produces splendid puppies. So much depends on how many you have to feed, but for a single dog this works very well. If alone a puppy may be difficult to feed, but with companions feeding is competitive. Give all that they can manage with enthusiasm and, when they seem to be not quite sure that they are hungry, take it away. Children are believed to develop better in the long run if not over-fed; dogs certainly do.

Puppies under ten weeks need special foods. Newborn pups can be reared on Cow & Gate baby food; it should be mixed a little stronger than is recommended for children of the same age and given about every three hours.

Young dogs

For young dogs the number of feeds is as follows:

8 to 12 weeks—4 to 5 feeds a day
12 to 16 weeks—3 to 4 feeds a day
16 to 26 weeks—2 feeds a day

Proprietary dog foods are expensive and their quality is not always satisfactory. Tripe, paunches and knackers' meat, if available, can all be used successfully. Flaked maize is one of the cheapest cereals for dogs, but flesh, vitamins and calcium (milk) are also essential. Certain special proteins, of which liver is the source, seem good for dogs and can be fed as a portion of their diet when training commences at 16 weeks or before. Dogs must eat something, and high value feed, even if expensive, has the advantage of being helpful in training and a desirable addition to the diet.

HEALTH

Look at the puppy. Is he energetic? Plump? Are his gums and tongue bright red? Is his tummy distended? Are there marked knobs on his ribs near the lower part of his chest? Are his limb bones thickened away from the 'elbow' (the joint two below his shoulder blade which points back) and towards the 'knee' (the one below the hip which points forward)?

Lethargy means serious ill-health; thinness—undernourishment; pallor—anaemia (more red meat needed); distended tummy—threadworms are likely. The growing ends of the bones become unduly thickened in rickets, which indicate a need for more calcium (milk) and cod liver oil (vitamin D). By contrast, increasing weight and size show that the animal is healthy.

These are guides intended to help diagnosis and indicate immediate treatment. If you find signs of illness, veterinary advice is essential.

Fleas and parasites

Very few dogs do not have some fleas, which may be a source of worms. Skin nits and types of mange are rather insidious. Flea powders and dips against these infestations are well worthwhile. Old kennels and their surrounding earth become infected. Veterinary advice should be sought.

Worms

All puppies seem to get round-worms and routine treatments are essential. The age at which these should be given is a matter for the veterinary surgeon. Tape-worm infestation is usually seen as segments in the motions; this, too, requires treatment.

Inoculations

The protective inoculations and the booster dose to follow against distemper, hard pad and the yellows are a 'must'. The veterinary surgeon will advise you as to the optimum age (probably twelve weeks) at which these should be given.

Page 35
(*above*) The recall signal
(and a sure way of attrac-
ting any puppy of any
breed); (*left*) Hand signal
for 'To Ho'.

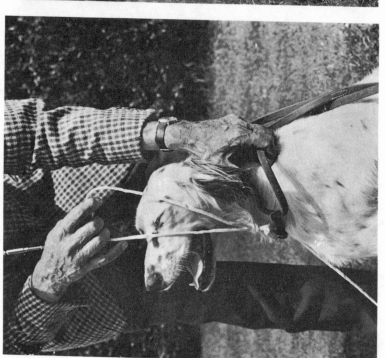

Page 36 (*left*) How to put the check cord through the slip lead so that the dog can be slipped unimpeded; (*right*) The hand loop of the slip lead on the right wrist, the check cord in the left hand

CHAPTER 3

First Lessons

You now have a puppy about four months old, which is disease-free, a third grown, and has lost one or two milk teeth. He should know his name and come when called, be perfectly friendly, and accustomed to his lead to the extent that he does not struggle to slip his collar backwards. No attempt has yet been made to stop him pulling on the lead or to make him walk to heel. Neither of these lessons is much fun for a puppy! Take him for walks and let him frolic about in suitable open spaces, then call him. He will usually come to be patted or bribed with a tit-bit, but get him to come without making too much fuss. Often kneeling down and opening your arms will bring a puppy crashing against your chest. He is too young for real discipline, although you may say 'No' to stop him doing things like getting on chairs or chewing boots. Dogs enjoy training and attention, but not being knocked about. The object is to inspire co-operation and enthusiasm, not fear.

In training, certain words and signals are used. It is preferable, though not essential, for the dog to learn the words of command before he develops the desire to hunt.

WORDS OF COMMAND

These should be short and unlikely to be used out of context—for example, 'Drop' not 'Down'.

1 No (don't do it)
2 Dead Dead (here is something nice)
3 To Ho (stop still)
4 On (go on)
5 Drop (lie or sit down)
6 Heel (stay behind)

These preliminary commands are verbal, thus allowing the handler to have both hands free without having to fumble for the whistle. In the later stages, these words of command are replaced by signs, gun shots and whistle signals.

Training should be fairly regular, the lessons being given on most days of the week and not exceeding ten minutes at a time—the limit of a dog's concentration. They should be conducted indoors in a familiar and often explored room, stable, garage or hard standing. There should be no distractions—from people, dogs, sparrows, blowing paper or other impediments to concentrated effort. The handler himself should be warm, comfortable and relaxed, with the requisite amount of time to spare. Be sure the pup

likes what he is doing, so that he becomes co-operative from the start. Before a meal is the best time to
begin.

STOPPING AT SPEED—THE 'TO HO' LESSON

The first lesson is to teach the dog to stop in full
career at the word of command 'To Ho'. The whole
point of the exercise is to check him at top speed—
after he has smelt game and *not before* he has started
to hunt. The object is for him to locate and point, but
not flush. I have so often seen pointing dogs who
stayed steady like retrievers at the handler's side and
whose whole training seemed to be directed to flushing when hunting. This distinction must be grasped
at the outset or the whole system fails and it is point-
less to continue training as described in this book.

This lesson must be carried out in stages and the
details are very important:

1   Take a cord about 18 feet in length, no
thicker than a pencil but not so thin as to cut your
hands. Tie a few knots in it to give you a grip.
Make a loop—not a noose—sufficiently large to
slip over the dog's head, but not so loose that he
can easily get out of it by pulling backwards. For
outdoor work, at a later stage in the lesson, a
plastic clothes-line or synthetic fibre cord, which
does not absorb water, will be useful.

2   Slip the cord over his head and allow him to

get used to trailing it about; a few minutes is usually enough.

3   Call him to you, holding the cord loosely in your hand with the free end trailing. Be careful not to tread on the slack.

4   About a dozen prepared baits—something the pup enjoys eating—should be ready to hand. Dog biscuits of the kind made in coloured shapes are clean, easy to throw and make a clatter on the floor. These seem to demonstrate, by the way, that a dog's vision is monochrome, as yellow and pink biscuits appear to be no easier for him to see on a dark floor than the black or brown ones. Not all dogs like these, and fried liver, dried and diced, is often more popular and not too messy to handle. Ordinary cooked meat or cheese, cut into squares rather smaller than sugar cubes, can also be used successfully. Larger baits will be needed later when working on grass.

5   Say 'Dead Dead'. Show the bait in your hand and bowl it underarm along the floor. The pup should see it and rush after it, trailing the cord over your hand. Do not check him inadvertently in this. The puppy must follow the hand movement and be eager to eat what is offered. Let him do this three or four times.

6   Again say 'Dead Dead', attract the dog's attention to the bait in your right hand and hold the cord loosely in your left. Bowl the bait along the ground and let the puppy start off after it. Then say 'To Ho' clearly and bring the dog to a

stop about 4 feet from the bait. The dog will strain at the cord, fuss, go left and right, but will be held back from the bait and, with a bit of luck, will become still or at any rate less mobile.

7   Then say 'On' and let the cord slip so that the puppy rushes on and eats the bait. He must start off after the bait and then stop. He should not sit beside you waiting for the command 'On'.

Now the handler is put to the test. He must not be careless and jerk the pup by inadvertently stepping on the cord, but must make sure it runs freely. Nor must he give the 'To Ho' command without being able to enforce it, that is, without being able to grip the cord. It is important for him to remember the principle that the pup must start after the bait before being stopped.

The use of the check cord

The check cord is a flexible instrument; it can be used lightly by slightly increasing the tension, or harshly by jerking the pup on to his back. If the dog is unresponsive to the cord when pulled gently, then his attention must be caught by jerking it, stopping him very sharply. Do not be too severe, but gentle and persistent. A most dramatic jerk can be given by letting the cord trail and then stepping on a knot. But watch what you are doing and try to put yourself in the dog's place. Self-criticism is no bad thing in dog training. This basic lesson should never be associated in the dog's mind with anything but pleasure; there should be no rows, no cross words.

It is very important to get all the details right. A dog can learn so much, especially the wrong thing. Slightly relaxing the tension on the cord before saying 'On' is a catch. Be sure the cord is still slightly resistant after the command 'On'.

This lesson, the 'To Ho' command, must be perfect. In a short time, sometimes after only five or six throws, the dog will stop on command, although some take very much longer to learn. Be sure he starts off eagerly and only stops at the command 'To Ho' and not by anticipating, through any change in tension on the cord, that he will be stopped. You have to be cunning about this or he will get things wrong. It must be the word and only the word. To stop in full chase must become a reflex action, over-riding all other considerations. This is what the 'To Ho' must be to your pupil.

Dogs learn from the pattern of events more easily than from words. The sequences in training should be varied. Stopping the dog as he runs after the bait should become progressively less frequent as he learns.

Throw the bait right and left as well as forward, so as to get him to follow hand direction, which will ultimately become the hand signals. As he gets more proficient, you must start him with the word 'On' and again stop him with the word 'To Ho'. Imagine he is hunting, when he will point and advance on command and stop at command on his way after the bird. This is to ensure that the dog does not flush without the gun keeping up with him. A glance at page 67 shows the need for the repeated stop and advance.

If he is showing signs of being aware of birds but not pointing, he can be stopped at command—the hand movements will start him hunting in the desired direction. He may tend to get in front of you before you throw and in this way be too quick on the bait for command. Stand so that you can throw either way, with the dog behind your throwing arm and not in front of it.

Once this basic lesson has become a drill—and a really good one—you can proceed to the next stage, the 'Drop'.

CHAPTER 4

Teaching the Signals

You have been commanding the dog and rewarding him, calling him and making a fuss of him, but now you command him without reward. The 'Drop' lesson is sometimes easy to teach and sometimes very difficult. Solitude and a confined space are a great help to a dog's concentration, but unless you can work in a big barn or garage you will have to move out of doors when longer distances are required. The dog must, of course, go for walks and during these you can try out the various commands as he learns them. Be sure you are in a position to enforce obedience with a check cord or he may learn to disregard commands in the open. If he gets no orders, he cannot disobey them!

THE DROP

Say 'Drop', raise your right hand and press him down with your left into a sitting position. Slowly back away with your right arm raised, enforcing the command with your voice and repeated pressure. Fairly soon you can stand 6 feet away from him dropped. Often he will respond very quickly to the raised arm alone.

Make sure this is drilled into him, and then attempt to walk away 15 yards. When he will stay dropped at this distance, call him to you and drop him again at half way.

Get him to respond to the hand signal alone. Follow this up with a whistle signal and raised hand, and then the whistle alone. Be careful to end the drop by calling him and not by just lowering the raised hand. The habit of starting to move once the hand comes down will be a nuisance later on, if you are caught up in a fence or doing something which requires the use of both hands.

Whistle signals

Whistle signals can be given as shown below, with many variations. It seems that the way you blow and not the whistle itself is what matters, except in the case of the silent whistle. You can change whistles at once; for instance, if you lose your own whistle and borrow one, the signal is still effective.

1   'Drop': short blast on a silent whistle; the 'Acme' is a popular model.
2   'Look back and turn': short blast, pause, short blast on ordinary whistle.

3 'Come back': continuous warbling note on ordinary whistle.

4 'On': 'tweet tweet' *and hand signal.*

Hand signals

Hand signals should invariably accompany the whistle signals.

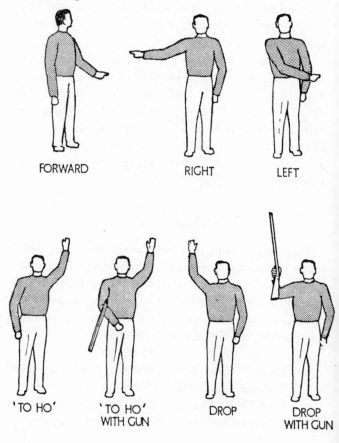

FORWARD   RIGHT   LEFT

'TO HO'   'TO HO' WITH GUN   DROP   DROP WITH GUN

The hand signals are the same as the gestures of throwing the bait in the initial lesson, but exaggerated: underhand swing for forward, right and left-swing for sideways.

Dropping to a noise

When the dog is looking away from you, clap your hands above your head, say 'Drop' and lower the left hand. Usually he drops without difficulty. Now replace the clap noise with a shot; a starting pistol can be used for this. The dog looks round, sees the raised hand and drops. If a gun is used, be sure he is some distance away the first time it is fired and shoot into the air in the opposite direction. A gun fired behind and past you sounds very loud, as you may find out if a friend goes out dogging with you! Do not shoot near the kennel, if you have other dogs. They do not like it and nervousness is infectious!

The drop drill

The drop drill can be summarised like this:

1 Drop him at your feet by words, pressure and signal.
2 Keep him dropped while you move away.
3 Drop him by word and signal.
4 Drop him by signal alone.
5 Drop him coming towards you by word and signal.
6 Drop him going away by word and signal.

47

7   Drop him by silent whistle and signal.
8   Drop him by silent whistle alone.
9   Catch his attention by clapping your hands and drop him by voice and signal.
10 Drop him by shot.

This drill should be carried out at increasing distances at home and on your walks. The need for it to be instantly obeyed is obvious. If you have difficulties as the range increases, the use of a 75-yard-long trailing check cord may be necessary (see page 50). Let him run about trailing the cord, which he already knows from his 'To Ho' lessons. Pick up the cord gently, give the command and, if necessary, enforce it by jerks and repeated commands.

Shot signal

Be sure to get the shot signal working really well long before he has birds shot to him. The shot is a command to stay still and not to look for a falling or flying bird! Carrying the gun or starting pistol is a nuisance and its use tends to be neglected in training, but it is important for the dog to become accustomed to it.

Another feature of the drop can now be discussed. Most people shoot from the right shoulder and the gun can be readily raised by the right hand to change the noise into the visual signal. The left hand can be raised for the 'To Ho' signal leaving the right to hold the gun point downwards.

If by starting early you have drilled all this into the dog before he really begins to hunt seriously, so much the better. As soon as he starts to look eagerly for small birds and to chase them, your difficulties will increase. The temptation to disobedience is so much greater and he can so easily get too far away.

REGULAR PRACTICE

Now practise the drop regularly and often and, if necessary, use the check cord to enforce obedience. The dog may too easily have the idea that he has to obey at home but not in new and exciting surroundings. Take him around the country and practise the drop. You can usually get permission to use a golf course or recently grazed fields, or those which have just been cut for silo or hay. At this stage you do not want game, just space.

All this time the original 'To Ho' lesson should be continued. When you let him out in the morning, or before feeding, throw a few baits, get him to 'To Ho', drop, and come when called. Use the whistle and signals. The whole drill can be done in ten minutes, if he does what he is told readily.

TURNING AND RETURNING

Without using the drop, try and drill the dog into turning on the whistle and returning to you on the whistle. Some dogs do so very readily, while others just will not, continuing to chase one lark after another. If you are training an easy dog, he looks up and follows the hand signal across, or comes to his name and the recall signal. This kind of dog usually learns to cross and re-cross in front of you without difficulty. Some dogs have a tendency to bore into the wind, which must be checked. They tend to get farther and farther out in front. If they are amenable to the drop, however, you steadily improve the pattern of hunting.

Technique of the long check cord

A check cord of 75 yards long can be used to enforce the turns, but remember that two or three turns or drops without the cord are far more valuable than obedience forced with the cord.

The technique of the long check cord is complex:

1 The cord should be light, strong, and of a substance which does not soak up water and thus become too heavy. Plastic clothes-line, nylon cord and what is sold to fishermen as 'cod' line are satisfactory. All will burn your hands unless you wear gloves.

2 The line needs to be kept on some form of reel. This can be made from two ordinary 12-inch school rulers and three cotton reels. Bore holes in the centre and 2 inches from each end of the rulers and fix the cotton reels with thin bolts into place to separate the two rulers. Two washers are used for the centre and a handle can be made out of bent metal protected by insulating tape. A suitable

piece of metal can usually be obtained from a garage.

3   Tie the line to a suitably sized dog collar. Loop the fastened collar over one of the projecting ends of a ruler and wind the cord on to the reel. When the cord is to be used, let the end trail and, holding the handle, allow the reel to spin as you walk leaving the cord in a straight line behind you. When the collar drops off the reel, you can fasten the collar to the dog's neck. The reel is light enough to carry in a pocket or haversack.

4   Buckle on the collar (which is attached to the check cord) behind the slip lead on the dog's neck. (When using a loop on the check cord, pass it through the slip lead from behind forwards and then over the dog's neck, so that it settles behind the slip lead.) When the lead is slipped over the dog's head to let him go, it is therefore free of the check cord. By placing the hand loop of the lead over the left wrist, the check cord on the palm of the left hand and taking the neck loop of the slip lead on your fingers, the dog is freed with lead dangling from your hand and the check cord gliding free over the palm, ready to be grasped. The right hand is thus kept free for the whistle and signals. (See illustrations on page 53.)

5   It is essential to wind up the cord tidily after use, starting with the collar end. Once tangled up it takes a long time to unravel. Keep the check cord free of knots, except for about three near the trailing end to warn you that you are running out of cord.

6   While the dog is going straight, the cord runs easily. Whistle and tighten your grip on the cord and, if necessary, jerk it to get him round. If he turns correctly, coming back straight across you, you can let the cord go when it runs out and catch it again as he passes you. This gives you a cast of nearly 50 yards to the side, while you still have the cord in your hand, when he is directly in front on the return cast. You then drop the cord and catch it again near the middle for the next turn.

7   If he bores into the wind, the friction, as you hold the cord, of his dragging the loop is much greater than while he is going correctly. Call him back and, the instant he begins to come towards you, let the cord glide once more, lessening the pull on the dog. He will learn to come across because the drag is so much less. It is important to start him across the wind so that he does not form a loop in the cord by going forward and then turning.

To demonstrate to yourself what happens at the dog's end of the cord, drive two sticks into the ground about 10 yards apart; walk, trailing the cord straight behind you, to the first stick; turn at right angles round it and again at the second stick, and walk back along a course parallel to the cord. It glides along quite easily. Now tie the end to a post, walk along the fence for 30 or 40 yards and turn in a wide circle. The pull is far greater when circling the fixed point. By means of increasing the tension, you

ge 53 (*above*) Hand loop and neck loop of the slip, with the check
rd able to run freely across the hand; (*below*) The gloved hand
th loop of slip and check cord across the palm. White burns of the
check cord can be seen across the fingers, hence the gloves

Page 54 (left) The correct position from which to shoot. Firing from behind may alarm the dog and

can encourage the dog to follow the desired path; he will learn quite fast.

It is hard work for a puppy on a check cord, so do not run him too long. Now is a good opportunity to keep him dropped for long periods while he recovers his breath.

If the dog has a strong scent, he will not turn, so he must be watched until there is the slightest indication that he is finding. Then either let him make it good and 'To Ho' him, or drop him and start hunting again. Hope that your lessons will start on very barren ground so that you can get the dog treating his ground correctly, even before he is hunting seriously, in some cases.

LESSONS LEARNED

At this stage the puppy's accomplishments are that he:

1 Answers his name
2 Comes to the whistle and signal
3 Is excited by 'Dead Dead', which attracts his attention
4 Stops at the command 'To Ho'
5 Follows the hand signal right, left and forward
6 Drops to (a) voice; (b) signal; (c) silent whistle; (d) hand clap; (e) shot
7 Can be turned by whistle and hand signal

He will do all these indoors except 6 (e) and 7, and will do them all out of doors at ranges up to 40 or 50 yards. None of the lessons will be quite perfect, but he will at least know. An older dog, though more difficult to teach some lessons, should have come along rather faster and be able to take more drill at a time.

WALKING TO HEEL

Your dog should now be taught to walk to heel on the lead. Hold him short on the lead in the left hand, and with the right swish a light stick in his face and say 'Heel'. I usually use a bit of willow herb as the stick. When he begins to get the idea, hold lead and stick in the left hand, letting the lead become looser and tapping him back as needed with the stick.

Do not make too much of walking him to heel loose. It can be a perfect pest if when he is upset he will not hunt or leave you, but just follows you about. It is true it relieves the handler a great deal by not having him pulling, and later conserves his energy out shooting, but it is not part of his hunting training.

CHAPTER 5

First Points

All this time you have probably been aching to get the dog pointing. There is no rush about this. If you are lucky and patient, you will have taught him the drill first. When the puppy is about nine months old, and possibly has pointed larks and small birds and an occasional game bird found by accident, you will try and get him pointing in earnest.

For a puppy born in January, February or March the only times are September, October and November. Pheasants can be used, though grouse or partridges are ideal. Later puppies, born in April, May, June or July, can be started on paired birds in February, March or April. Those born from August to the end of the year are better left until July and started on the young grouse. Dogs convert very easily from partridges to grouse and quite rapidly from grouse to partridges. It seems that grouse leave a stronger scent.

Aim at perfect conditions to help him. These are:

1   A nice day with a warm, moist wind
2   An area with plenty of birds
3   Enough cover to hold the birds

A GOOD START

Having found favourable conditions, take the pup out alone if you can. Depending on his tractability, run him free or on the check cord. If he comes of a good pointing family, he should show some indication of finding and should stop on the command 'To Ho' or quite spontaneously. Approach him very quietly, wait while you count ten and get him to move in on the birds, if possible with your fingers touching his neck behind the ears. When the birds flush, say 'Drop' sharply and press him down. You must be most patient and persevering in roading the birds up. It is most upsetting to both of you if they get up just as you feel that there is nothing there. If all works according to plan, make much of the dog to show you are pleased. Put him on the lead and move to the haunt. He will rather disgustingly eat the droppings the birds have left. It seems quite harmless to his health. Now stop and wait for a bit to show him the incident is over, then start him off again.

Some people are apt to draw forward at this moment, but remember that you do not want an accidental flush which may happen on unhunted ground. Two or three casts are preferable before the next find. Ground on which birds are very scarce makes puppies dwell on the haunt because they cannot find elsewhere. If the dog dwells on the old scent and haunts, do not make a noise or fuss. Say quietly 'On, On' and let him convince himself that the place is clear. He will then start hunting again and you will soon find he learns to go on and seek fresh adventures.

If you have real luck this first day you may get three or four points quickly and accurately. This is enough. Hunt any dog too long and he makes some mistake. This does not matter with a made dog, but will unsettle a puppy. Gradually let the dog have more freedom to range and find, but at first try to keep him close, where control is easier.

Two or three days with plenty of birds and no accidents often make a dog for life. They may go on in days from the first point to running creditably in a puppy stake, completely unperturbed by running with another dog and all the strangeness and excitement of a field trial.

INITIAL MISTAKES

Your first day may not go like this. The young dog may gallop about wildly, and flush and chase. This failure may come from handling mistakes—firstly, letting the dog go too wide and too far forward all through training; secondly, not recognising instantly that he is feathering on birds, and helping by steadying him; and, lastly, by not believing him when he points. From inexperience he may point very far back from birds—on the foot scent, in fact—and for the same reason may road either too slowly or too fast, often starting too slow and ending with a rush. You may give up and make a fresh cast right into birds. Any of these happenings upsets the puppy. The only thing to do is to use the check cord and see if you can get it right. If he persists in boring into wind and not hunting the ground, call the whole thing off for a week or two and go back to the old lessons, concentrating on the beat.

Be sure to have shots as soon as you are getting some confidence in him. It is useful to have someone to fire for you about 30 yards away. To the dog it should be just another bang, meaning 'Drop'. Remember he has heard the noise before and been drilled to drop to it under the same circumstances. Forget the bird and the gun. After all he may miss! Do not try and shoot anything to him for a few days at least, and then only when you are right with the dog, possibly with a hand or a check cord on him.

Patience is now required, in waiting for the opportunity to have a hunting day and in insisting on the ground treatment which gives you a chance to intervene effectively.

Faults which occur at this stage of training and development of a puppy are bolting off and chasing anything that moves, such as small birds. The puppy forgets everything in the excitement of pursuit and may give tongue. This is less likely to occur if he has had plenty of freedom at an early age to learn that he cannot catch swallows. It needs checking—by jerking him over with the cord, if necessary—as it could be the greatest nuisance.

CORRECTING FAULTS

Until now the need for punishment has been avoided as far as possible. All commands have been enforced with the check cord. Now you have a condition which you would like to stop without using the check cord, especially if the dog seems to be learning to behave on the cord and go his own sweet way when freed. Look at the situation from his point of view. He has been happily chasing, oblivious of any background noises; he is a bit blown, tired and probably lost. He returns to master—to blasts of the whistle and a beating. It adds up in his mind to keeping away when the whistle is blown.

Now, if your training works, drop him, walk away, wait, blow the whistle and get him to come to you. Put him on the lead and give him a short rest, while you get ready for trouble. Find a nice dry clod, or some suitable missile like a rolled up dog lead, or carry a light stick, and hold the whistle in your teeth. Slip him off, let him take about four jumps, then blow the whistle and instantly throw the missile at him. If you make anything of a good aim, he will look back surprised and with his attention caught. Then roar out his name, signalling him across in front of you.

It is only in this situation that the male handler has an advantage, as his voice is louder than a woman's and he may have had more practice in throwing things! It is hoped that the pup is deeply impressed by this scene and will respond after passing in front of you. Let him continue his cast a short distance, whistle and call, and again throw things if needed to get the second turn. Then let him cast more normally and turn him again. A hedge or some barrier may help with this third turn.

The advantage of having restricted the puppy's beat and turning him close to you now becomes evident. He has been turned before at 20 yards and will turn, on the whistle and shout, at 15 yards this time. Let him gradually get back to his range of about 40 yards and then again, suitably armed, blow and shout just after he has passed you and, if necessary, throw when he is near enough for a possible hit.

If this method fails, you must try hitting him with the stick. If he gets away and does not respond to name or whistle, stand still and do nothing. When he is fairly close, blow the whistle, shout at him, catch him and hit him twice. Continue to make a scene for a bit, put him on the check cord, get him started and turn him with the whistle and immediately jerk a couple of times. Then let the cord trail unheld and see if you can get him round on the whistle. If this fails, the only thing is to drop him on the check cord at about 20 yards, whistle and signal him back. Perseverence will win but it is going to take weeks.

If the cause of each bolt is a chase after a small bird or game, it is much easier to correct; but if it is a mad galloping about without hunting it will take time. No dog can hunt going at full speed and needs to travel at about three-quarter speed, using his nose and mind to find something. It is obvious to the experienced observer that some dogs, in the words of an American authority, are simply 'galloping to hear their bones rattle', not questing for game, just enjoying speed and activity. This may only last for a half cast or so, but sometimes is continuous. These dogs are always prone to flush and generally get out of hand.

Once you are beginning to have confidence in your dog's pointing and hunting, take him on to more barren ground so that he can learn to search and find. There is little need for locating a dog on ground that is teeming with game and he needs to get to the conditions he will normally work under.

PROBLEMS TO OVERCOME

Sheep

Sheep are found on all grouse moors and dogs should be introduced to them. The 'valley' sheep of the English countryside do not seem to smell the same as moorland sheep. A dog which appears uninterested in sheep in a grass field may behave badly on the moors.

Often a puppy goes to look at a sheep—an action which simply terrifies the handler—but he usually turns away at once on command. If this happens, you may be quite safe for the future. Do not run two dogs on the moor until you are pretty sure that both are steady to sheep.

On two occasions I have had sheep chases following a 'back' of the sheep. It is quite an understandable mistake on the part of both dog and handler. In running, the dog backs a sheep which stands watching him; the handler comes up and says, 'Get on, you fool', and the dog gets on after the now running sheep. I am afraid that beating the dog is necessary after a sheep chase, and is usually more likely to be effective because you get to the dog holding the sheep. With hares it is quite different; if the dog is beaten when he comes back from chasing a hare, it is unlikely he will get the message.

Hares

Hares are a very thorny problem. You must hope not to meet them in the early stages of pointing birds; once the dog is interested in birds, he is less likely to worry about hares.

Deliberately going out to break a dog off hares may only draw his attention to them. However, if they are plentiful, it simply has to be done. Check him repeatedly and use the check cord. Since you would prefer him to take no notice of them at all, drawing his attention to every distant hare and dropping him is hardly likely to achieve this. Should a dog get 'hare minded', he looks for them and hunts for them. Wherever he goes, hares appear in all directions. I believe the explanation is that most dogs hunt past a large proportion of the hares in the area.

A similar difficulty may occur with dogs trained on pheasants. The dog learns to follow the lines instead of hunting the ground. His success confirms his belief that this is the simplest way to find, and he may disregard partridges to get on with the pheasant lines. I am not referring to long roads after a dog has pointed, but to going off huge distances on a line without pointing.

CHAPTER 6

The Beat

I would like here to restate the question of beat:

1 A regular pattern of hunting with the correct advance must find most birds in the long run. The pattern should be varied to suit conditions.

2 A controlled beat is the greatest help in the early training.

3 To give a puppy the best chance, he must beat into wind.

4 The beat is the most difficult thing to establish; therefore the greatest efforts should be made to get the detail correct from the very beginning.

FLUSHING is of two kinds—the accidental blundering into birds which are down wind and cannot be found, and the failure to stop soon enough when the birds are scented. Both can be corrected by the handler who has sufficient control.

DROPPING TO WING is learnt by correct points

66

giving the handler every opportunity to drop the dog as the birds take off.

ROADING is learnt by following up after correct points.

STICKINESS—the failure to road fast enough and readily enough—comes from flushing, leading to over emphasis on the drop to wing and inborn tendency to dwelling on the point. Only great patience can overcome it. Coax the dog on by leading or lifting gently. Some dogs are sticky to the haunt and then follow on the line much better. This tendency may make them sticky going to a haunt from which the birds have flown unseen, and so give them the reputation for false pointing. Walking past the point and calling the dog on may get him forward. Leading him on, and then putting your fingers to simulate the pressure of the lead behind his ears, may work. I am inclined to think that the best method is to stand still in the hope the scent will lessen with time and the dog go on to regain it. Stickiness can be cured, but it is a fault much easier to correct in the absence of spectators. When watched, the handler is more likely to become irritated and show it.

CREEPING IN ON POINT seems to be due to the birds moving away from the pointing dog. This is far more likely to happen if the handler fails to approach stealthily and slowly. Running or hurrying to the point is most unwise. Approach very slowly and quietly, and check the slightest movement with the silent whistle signal or 'To Ho'. Usually the very first indication of the creep forward is a change from the

67

rigid tail to feathering. I am confident that this indicates that the birds are restless.

IMPROVING THE DOG'S BEAT

The perfect beat has been illustrated in Chapter 1. Diagrams 1, 2 and 3 below give further guidance:

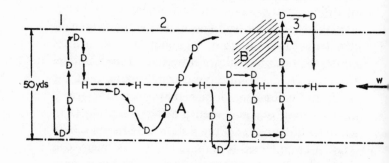

1   Ideal method and distance: 40 yards right and left, advance 15 yards

2   Boring into wind: getting 100 yards in front of handler. Birds can be flushed on unhunted ground

3   Irregular beat: too far away to the side; missing ground. Again flushing is easy

Flush and danger of chases can occur when the birds cannot be smelt down wind. In diagram 2 the handler is being rapidly left behind and at point A contact with the dog is lost. In diagram 3 contact is lessened at point A, but the real danger is that birds may be bumped into in the unhunted area B.

68

Dogs can only get the body scent up to 25 yards and no more. With a puppy, any forward advance above this distance is a fault that can lead to trouble by causing flushing. Field trial champions can manage a bigger advance, because they are aware from the complete absence of any bird scent that the area is blank, but you are trying to help your puppy on populated ground. Boring into wind to any great extent is a fault which will result in birds being missed.

As the dog gains experience, certain tricks can be used to improve his beat. The first is the use of a cheek wind as already illustrated on page 24. The dog's course is in front of you on the more up-wind cast and behind you on the more down-wind cast, and to cover the same beat by the diagonals that he makes he has to go about one-sixth farther than on a head wind. If he tends to pass too far in front, you can bear away from him as he goes behind you, easily attract his attention as he comes back to you and signal him in more closely. It is the same as he goes on the up-wind side. If he does not advance enough on each cast, you can turn into wind and signal him more forward. The fact that he has a greater distance to go allows you this change of direction and pace more easily.

HUNTING DOWN WIND

No mention has been made of hunting a dog down wind. A dog that bores into wind may be constantly drawn into wind by slight touches of scent and not by a desire to get away from you. Hunted down wind this tendency may keep drawing him back in your direction and enable you to keep contact and steer him across in front of you.

Hunting down wind is a useful manoeuvre out shooting, but for the reason now described is not suitable for early training. When the gun or guns are moving over the beat, game tends to move away from them. If the dog beats his ground by the normal up-wind method, he constantly points the haunt or inadvertently flushes the game down wind of his path. He must get out much farther and loop round the game, which is between the dog and the handler, who walks straight down so that he and the dog end up facing one another, about 20 yards apart.

You may be able to get the dog to come in to meet you, but because the game tends to run back towards him he is often sticky. Whatever happens, the handler slowly advances on the dog and may be rewarded by the birds flushing between them and very close. Make the 'Drop' signs and signals, and keep him down. If nothing happens, start roading. The handler may have passed the birds or they may have run to one side and behind the dog. He may be able to follow the birds up or he may lose them and have to make another down-wind cast. Some dogs become quite brilliant at this, going down wind, using the diagonal track of the birds to make it a cheek wind for the next point. This is a very good way of getting near wild birds late in the season. The handler must

age 71 Matters of style. (*above*) An English setter in the classic
oint position, head raised to confirm game scent up wind; (*below*)
 pointer in the same attitude. Note the flews parted to taste the air

Page 72   The set and the point. The English setter drops, the pointer stands

not attempt to circle the dog. He goes to him the shortest way, trying to get the quarry between them.

At this stage of improving the dog's beat, I am talking in terms of larks drawing him into wind, and a flush is not going to cause the handler much worry. The dog should be on the check cord when working down wind. Sometimes these attempts work very well and quickly. I am sure most dogs wish to please if you can only put the correct ideas across.

ERRORS IN TRAINING

Another fault is circling and turning down wind. A dog which is hunting should turn into the wind, always questing for the body scent. Some go out, turn in a circle and return to their handler completely failing to beat the ground in a logical manner. I believe this is due to the handler not insisting from the beginning on the dog crossing the wind at right angles to its direction. If a dog is cast directly into wind and asked to turn, he may well turn back to his handler. This is far better than not turning at all, but may lead to this circling and down-wind turning.

Suppose you have a fence at right angles to the wind, insist on the puppy going along it and then turning. Do not let him go straight into wind and then turn across it. He may only make one backward cast, but he is always liable to circle and spoil your chances.

This seems so obvious, but it is difficult to prevent and is sometimes disregarded by the handler. I am

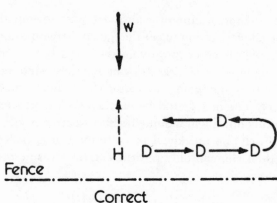

Correct

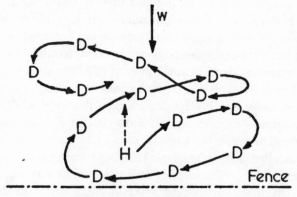

Incorrect, wasting
energy and flushing

sure that going for the correct beat makes for sim-
plicity. If you disregard it and rush into pointing,
then trouble comes.

Another thing that handlers do is to walk forward

into the beat. I cannot understand why they do it, especially in fenced areas. If you come into a field at the corner, hug the down-wind fence until you have gone far enough to start and then send the dog along the fence. His first half-cast makes that area good and you have disturbed the other half-cast by walking along it. If you bore out into the field, game is pushed back to the hedge behind you and the dog may well learn to cut back to make the hedge good or have a down-wind flush. Your job is to make him beat the field so that no mistake is likely.

HAWKING

The incurably sticky dog has one possible future. It is in hawking. Dogs are of great assistance here. It is a great thrill to run a dog with the hawk 'waiting on' —that is, taking great swoops over her master's head. You hear the trilling of her bells and the hiss of her passage as she crosses above you. The trick from the dog handler's point of view is to get the flush just as she turns back towards the point, when she has the position and distance to develop speed. It is all most dramatic and exciting. There are snags, however. One inevitable item is the wild spaniel which all falconers have around; another is the delay in getting hawks back after they have missed. They often go and sit sulking in distant trees. Dogs can help the short-winged hawks when rabbits or hares are plentiful. These hawks are carried until the game is afoot and then flown off the fist.

75

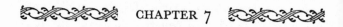

CHAPTER 7

Shooting Over Dogs

Now, supposing that in August or September you have a puppy which will do the basic work:

1   His range is fair.
2   He points staunchly.
3   He is steady to wing and shot.
4   He roads up satisfactorily.
5   He has possibly seen a bird shot.
6   He backs at least on command.

This is the moment when he can be allowed to run out shooting.

It is a great advantage to the handler to shoot over his dogs. Handlers who do not shoot have what they feel is a critical audience for their first shots; dogs are very sensitive to emotion on the part of the handler. However, if you are shooting, you have to concentrate at the time of the flush on the shot, not the dog. It cuts both ways.

If he is under 18 months old, do not take him out

76

shooting seriously, as he will become tired and careless. Take him out and give him four points, shooting
only when everything is right: (a) the handler is on
top of him; (b) a bird can be killed; (c) he is not
tired; (d) the half hour which he is run is directed
to his interest and nothing else.

If this is not acceptable, keep him at home until
next year. A successful point and shot marred by
some small dog failure is allowed to pass unrebuked
on a shooting day, while a failure in the shooting is
visited on the dog. A fair stint out shooting will improve a physically fully developed dog, but it is too
much for a puppy under two years old. Overworked
dogs show a lack of spirit in their work.

RUNNING IN TO THE FALL

Running in to the fall of the bird is a perfect curse.
Even if I am shooting I like for a few days to put
leads on the dog when I reach him and before I fire.
By having a short lead tied to the cartridge belt with
a loop to slip over his head you can enforce the drop.
Allowing pointing puppies to retrieve increases the
temptation to run in on the fall.

Your dogs should be encouraged to point dead.
When just one bird has been killed, be certain it is
dead and some little way out, put your dog on the
lead, walk a few yards and cast him down wind of
the bird. He will usually point it but, if he does not,
drop him and coax him forward until he does. Get
him to road to within a yard of the bird; then very

gently pick it up and let him smell it. Keep it in both hands, not dangling from the neck. Not infrequently this pointing dead happens quite spontaneously with birds which have gone on and died out of sight of the guns.

THE QUARRY

Some knowledge of the habits of the quarry is helpful. Pheasants tend to run and keep on running, especially if heading for home in a wood or hedgerow. This may make for very long and unsuccessful roads by young dogs. It also leads to dogs following up the ground scent without pointing, getting too far away, and even flushing.

Partridges are ideal, being in convoys, and flushing easily. However, if they are on very bare ground, sunning themselves or getting out of the wet, they may have to be manoeuvred into suitable cover for the dog to get close to them. Grouse are also ideal, but tend to vary their position on the moor according to the wetness or otherwise of the ground, the weather conditions of the day, and the opportunity to feed on blueberries, grass seeds and young heather.

A dog constantly drawing uphill to blueberries or downhill to wet ground may be caused to flush by this movement of the birds. Experts, more especially local ones, can successfully forecast the productive areas. Selecting suitable and productive ground is helpful, but a failure to realise why a puppy is edging away from you may cause much worse trouble. Hardly any dog will turn in the act of finding. If the dog's manner and direction suggest he is getting close to birds, do not try and turn him. This is the time when a knowledge of the likely places is most helpful. Experience alone will teach the handler. The most important thing is to watch the dog's actions and remember that the pattern was the same before previous flushes and points. Watch, try to remember, and be self-critical. It is a partnership, after all!

BLINKING

A fault which may develop just as you start shooting seriously is 'blinking' points. This consists of the dog pointing correctly, then leaving his point and often coming to heel. Usually he will advance with the handler and road in a timid and uncertain manner. The cure is no noise when the birds flush. No shooting, no 'Drop', no whistle.

The fault develops either from too much fuss when the dog is unsteady to flush or from a type of gun shyness. I once saw it caused in this manner. A dog pointed within about six jumps from being slipped. He was downhill of the guns. Unfortunately I had allowed four guns to come out. It was the first point of the day; as we moved, a covey got up below and beyond the dog. Standing shoulder to shoulder, the guns fired eight shots very close over the dog. He dashed back behind me and did the same thing as we came up to the next point. I got the guns to co-operate and pass the dog the third time, soothed him by talking quietly and slowly brought him forward. It worked all right and he seemed cured, but now and again, especially if anything went wrong, he would 'blink'.

Another dog would occasionally blink if the birds ran. This I blamed on harshness in correcting flushing. The dog's reasoning was that he would be blamed because the birds did not sit. He had been apt to creep in on running birds during his training.

BACKING

Until now you have worked your pup alone. I do not believe a companion is helpful in the early stages. There is one exception—pups will follow their mother and turn when she turns. If you can get the whole family out and turn the bitch, the pups being left behind learn to anticipate her turning themselves on the whistle. It is a very pretty sight if nothing more.

Once the pup is pointing, turning, dropping and fairly steady, you can take him out with a reliable companion. I do not think dogs learn by example. He should learn not to follow the other dog and to work independently as if the other dog were not there. Backing is stopping when he sees another dog on point. Some dogs are natural backers and do it automatically. Others look for the back and do no work; if you see a tendency to this, work him alone. He may be cured, but too often it means a lack of drive and ability. If the dog is at all obedient, you

can drop him once you are sure he can see the other
dog. Remember his horizon is limited and is not that
of a 6-foot man, and that he is using his nose to
locate birds, not looking out for his companion to
find them.

A good dog will learn to back quite readily. Some
very jealous dogs may be difficult. Dogs which steal
points are a nuisance, but the dog that looks for the
back is a dead loss. When teaching backing be sure
that the other dog is very genuine, roads quickly and
gets close to game before stopping. If your dog fails
to stop at command, he may stop by pointing behind
the other dog. Be certain that the pointing dog is
visible to your pupil and that he gets birds away.

BRACE WORK

The ultimate in pointer and setter work is the brace.
It can be defined as working two dogs to do the
ground faster and more thoroughly than one dog.
Imagine the two dogs beating the ground on opposite courses and advancing between beats twice as
far as a single dog. The ground would still all be
hunted and the handler allowed to walk twice as
fast, but he does not want to do this, so he encourages
a wider range.

If the normal beat is 112 yards on either side, the
handler now expects about 200 yards and a forward
advance of 50 yards. He walks 50 yards while the dog,
going ten times as fast, does 500; so the dog goes out
220 yards, forward 50 yards, and back 220 yards.

It is never exactly like this, but a good natural brace gets quite near it. The dogs both leave the handler level with him and turn, meeting in front of him, each aware that some ground has been hunted by the approaching dog. So, after meeting, they bore into the wind to get fresh ground but maintain their cross-wind path fairly accurately. They learn to go out more, partly from the handler's encouragement and partly because he only turns them very far out. The pattern becomes a series of flat St Andrew's crosses, the centre being hunted a little too close and the flanks about right.

The dogs do not make the theoretical advance or distance. They must be of the same pace and not be too jealous of one another. Mother and son, or father and daughter often make ideal braces. Braces are born, not made, because the speed factor is so important. Backing has to be automatic and held until commanded to start again, however far the handler and brace-mate road. Dropping to shot must be automatic and hunting recommenced by whistle signal.

Brace work is a great sight, and gives a wonderful feeling of achievement. It is a most effective way of shooting in suitable places. The ground must be flat, to enable the dogs to have a good view of one another; broken ground is hopeless. A dog's eyes are only about 24 inches from the ground when he is going. Measure off 2 feet on a stick and bring your eye down to that level. It is astonishing how limited your horizon becomes.

In practice you take the leads off and pocket them. Start one dog left by name and signal and then the other right. You occasionally whistle the turn to keep the beat correct. Shoot, pick up your bird while the brace stays dropped. Load up and whistle the 'tweet tweet' on signal, not messing about with leads etc, until you finally pick up.

For shooting parties, brace work has two disadvantages—your best dogs are together, and points and backs may cause confusion amongst the guns. Be grateful you have two such dogs, use them for your own amusement and in competition. They will be nearly unbeatable.

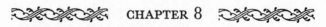

CHAPTER 8

The Handler and His Dog

THE TRAINED DOG

At the end of his first year you hope to have a full-grown dog which has been trained. If he was born in January, his training will have followed this course: domestication during March and April; indoor training in the commands in May and June, and outdoor training on the same lines in July and August. September has been devoted to concentration on the beat and, at the end of the month, if he is sufficiently forward, some points. At the end of September, or in October, a special attempt will have been made to get points in the most favourable conditions. Then follows a complete refresher course of indoor and outdoor training through the winter, with emphasis on the drop and the beat.

In the spring give the dog a course of paired birds and possibly a run in a puppy stake at a field trial in April. In May and June continue with the training, but try to get the dog well fleshed though fit, with slow work. He will be eighteen months old in July and can have serious training on grouse and another run in a puppy stake. If opportunities are favourable, he can have a few very short shooting days in August, September and October. Training in brace work can then begin.

Dogs which are given a hard season before they are twenty-four months old often work badly from fatigue and show the effects of it all their life. My definition of a hard season would be, say, going to Scotland and being worked five days a week from 12 August until about 7 September. This entails about twenty days real hard work. A younger dog could well do about six days in the same time.

Never work dogs too long. People have boasted to me that their dogs work five or six hours a day. You can usually tell this from their speed and relative lack of enthusiasm and the mistakes they make. Tired dogs do not slow down to start with. They go harder at it, but make mistakes; then slow and lose their beat and style. It takes them about five days to recover from such an experience.

In the dog's second season at twenty-six months old, it is time for another course on paired birds. In August, aged thirty months, the dog should be fit for full work and with luck will remain fit for the next six to eight years, reaching his peak at about six years old.

TEACHING AN OLDER DOG

The training of an adult dog presents some special problems. He must go through the period of domestication. This is important, although he may hate the sight of you for a bit. I heard of a retriever that was bought, shoved into a car for a couple of hours, and then let out on a dark moor; it vanished without trace. It is very important to get the dog to know and like you. The initial indoor training is essential as part of this process. It may only take a few days, but be certain he has the commands.

When he is friendly, pleased to see you, comes when called indoors, 'To Ho's' and drops to word, whistle and signal, then take him out and let him loose. He may walk to heel when asked, dash away when encouraged, return when called and point steadily. He may range correctly and will, in fact, be a made dog. If he comes from abroad, he will show the training and experience he has gained by going very wide and fast or even from one wood to the next.

If untrained, he will need all the range training, almost certainly with the check cord, and will show obvious faults, such as chasing. The system is the same as with a young dog, but remember it takes much longer to eradicate a fault than prevent it. The adult dog's sheer strength and speed may make him more difficult to train than a puppy. However, I have found that, provided you take trouble over the initial lessons, you can win.

The effort may be much less or much more, and the results still depend on the dog. When I started to train pointing dogs, following the instructions in a book, I believed that it all depended on the training. Certainly I had only one dog, boundless enthusiasm and energy, and just sufficient leisure to work on him regularly without overdoing it. A few years later I began to realise how intelligent and co-operative he had been. I had had the luck to get a 'superdog' with everything to start me off. You can give the dog opportunity, but he must give something too.

Dogs which are old enough to hunt before training starts, especially if they have done some self-hunting without proper control, usually learn their initial lessons as easily as any other dog; but the greatest care is needed in getting them across out of doors when there is something to find. It may be necessary to run them for much longer at a time in order to get the response to the drop.

A curious thing about dog development is that it seems to go in jerks. He got it nearly right all last month and then suddenly he has got it for all time. He drops without a word at the flush one day and then every day until the end of his life. So stick to it and suddenly you may find you are there!

A DOG'S REASONING

One of the greatest traps in dog training is thinking that dogs reason in the same way as the handler.

Dogs do not reason deductively in the same way. I am certain that their chain of thought is not: 'Master has blown the whistle; master is angry; I have done something wrong, what was it? I must not do it again.' I think a dog's thought process goes like this: 'Master is angry so I had better keep away.' Dogs do learn from immediate effects, such as the whistle, pull on the check cord and signal to turn. I am sure that they also appreciate certain things, such as the advantage of the forward cast and position when hunting with another dog.

Several dogs I have known always ran against another dog trying to be just into wind and just in front of the other dog. I am sure they knew that this way they got the points. I do not think they reasoned it out, they just experienced it and did it.

I am sure that dogs know that they point, you shoot, the bird falls and that you are pleased when this happens, and that your pleasure pleases them and your annoyance at missed birds upsets them.

I once had a setter which I took out flighting pigeons. His value was not the retrieving so much as his ability to hear, or at least know, when birds were coming and from what direction. He sat and turned his head towards them long before I was aware of anything coming. If I missed the first few shots he would dig a hole and go to sleep in it! He was certain that I was not trying. 'No retrieving so why bother' seemed to be the way he looked at it.

In training one must be sure that the dog understands. He will not reason back beyond the immediately preceding event. If he chases a hare and is beaten when he comes back, he probably thinks he is beaten for coming back. The fuss must be made as he takes off. For this reason the two stop signals must be perfect and when he stops or drops on command nothing except words are helpful.

Dogs are very sensitive to emotion and field trial nerves affect them, via the handler. People who fear dogs, frighten them and are likely to get bitten, while the person who has no fear of them is far safer. I do not think it is the dog's sense of smell that tells him of the handler's emotion, but the handler's manner. If you can *behave* normally it does not matter what you feel. I also think a dog that has never had a clout is inattentive, but a beaten-up dog is stupid from fear.

THE WELL-BEHAVED DOG

I have been keen on shooting and the countryside all my life and I have always found that a dog increased my pleasure. I have also found that other people's dogs did not invariably increase my enjoyment. A well-trained, brilliant dog is always a pleasure to watch. An ill-mannered dog is not. Dog training is fascinating to the trainer, but becomes a bore to the spectator rather quickly, and distressing if associated with a lot of noise. Accidents will happen and one should be tolerant, but it is also necessary to be considerate when taking dogs out with other people to ensure that their pleasure is not spoilt. If this training is followed, I think you will find everyone happy.

DO'S AND DONT'S

Do trust your dog when he finds.
Do conceal your emotions, if you possibly can.
Do imagine yourself in the dog's position.

Don't beat or frighten a dog when he returns to you.
Don't beat a dog who has dropped.
Don't rush to the point.
Don't leave the guns behind you, which is most alarming.
Don't work a dog in front of a line of guns walking; it is unnecessary, unhelpful, dangerous and a bore.
Don't go out on a very windy day (with apologies to Mr Jorrocks).

CHAPTER 9

On the Moor

The shooting season starts in August with grouse, and grouse moors are quite ideal for the pointing dogs. The season for pointing comes to an end in the first week in September when the birds become frustratingly wild and hard to approach. In September and October, partridges are the quarry if there are any around. By refraining from shooting at any covey exceeding four birds, only old and barren birds are killed, which seems to be a good thing for the stock.

Pheasants can be pointed from October to the end of the year. Again, taking care only to shoot adult cock birds or wanderers far from the covers seems quite helpful to the stock. Ducks can be pointed on a river and stalked with some success, by the handler keeping far enough away from the bank to be unseen and the dog pointing a little way back from the bank. Snipe and woodcock can be found in frosty weather where springs or other conditions produce areas of soft feeding ground. The bag is usually small, but it is a thrilling way of spending an hour or two if you have the opportunity.

THE TEAM

The ideal team for a hard season on the moor is five dogs, each run for 35 minutes between 10 am and 1 pm and for 25 minutes between 2 pm and 4 pm. They should do some walking before 10 am and after 4 pm. Such a team can go on day after day working perfectly, and this allows some latitude for one dog not being fit, such as a bitch on heat, or from some accidental cause. The team should have one or two crafty old warriors, two or three proved, vigorous dogs and one or two first season dogs.

The fewer the birds, the harder on the dogs and the guns. All are constantly on the move without rest for picking up and pointing.

Costs

It is hard to evaluate the cost of a team, which may take years to produce.

The most expensive method would include the following items:

		£
1	Handler at £1,000 pa, with house	1,050
2	Food at 20p a week (5 × 20 × 52)	52
3	Training ground: 1,000 acres at 20p an acre	200
		1,302

20 days in August and September: £65.10 a day.

If, however, handling is a hobby:

		£
1	Food (three times as expensive because partially prepared)	156
2	Training ground: 1,000 acres at 20p per acre	200
		356

20 days in August and September:
£17.80 a day.

If there are three guns out, the cost is therefore either £21.70 or £5.93 each.
If you entertain sixty guns and have six days' driving, with twelve beaters at £2.00 a day, the cost is £144.00, or £24.00 a day.

If the moor produces 100 brace a season dogging, it should produce five brace a day, or 3·3 birds per gun. Driving, it should produce 16½ brace a day, again 3·3 birds per gun. Four drives means some blank stands for some guns. At least the dogging guns get more contact. If the bag is four times as big, each gun gets thirteen birds—a splendid day's dogging, but not too outstanding driving. With more than 400 brace, driving has it every time. Of course, this is not what is possible. Mist, gales and rain all affect the bag as does the date. I would say that under 400 brace, much more fun can be had with the dogs. The handler who is doing it as a hobby also has

93

the fun of others shooting over the dogs, possible field trials and the general interest.

A SHOOTING DAY

For a host, a driving day is beset with anxiety, but can give the greatest pleasure when all has gone reasonably well and according to plan. For the dog handler, the anxieties are also there and the pleasure just as acute. Before breakfast, go out to see the weather and the dogs. After breakfast, which you have been far too worried to enjoy properly, load up the dogs, anxiously checking leads, whistle and possibly gun and cartridges.

At the meeting place, all seems well; only two guns, so you are to shoot! Only two other dogs, both labradors; one the gillie will lead, the other is a pup whose owner has a loud voice to which the pup pays little heed. Tactfully stress the danger and temptations of the pointing team leading the pup astray, at least at first, and get him on the lead too.

You then decide gloomily that the wind is too light and variable and that failures will be blamed on you and the dogs. Make up your mind to have the youngest first because he pulls so when away from you. Explain the procedure to the gun who has no experience of dogging.

You slip the dog across the wind. He is out like a bomb, but he is hunting not just racing, has turned automatically, and nice and short. By the third cast, he is going wide and well. Is it going to be a blank day? No sign of birds that you can see, but his head goes up and he points.

Walking very slowly to let the guns get into position as you approach, a whispered 'On On' and he boldly advances. 'Go back, go back,' is heard from the old cock as he rises. Are they never going to shoot! Shots right and left, and he still goes on. Three more birds much closer to the dog; one down and another missed, one is still easily in shot and to your huge relief you get him. The dog is still pointing stiffly. Load up! Load up! There's another. He roads on, turning left, and four more spring right under the guns' feet swerving like mad; another miss and then a fine shot. Three down, one each.

The labrador puppy finds one; the keeper's dog finds one, and your old faithful who has never stirred finds one. Everyone is pleased, the day is made. They all work well and by lunch the guns really come into position intelligently.

THE GUNS

Never have more than three guns; insist that they keep together with you (the handler), and take up the appropriate positions for each point. Guns spread out in line cause unnecessary disturbance and tend to get bored if they have the unproductive portion of the beat. The ideal party for the pointing day is three guns. Get them to take numbers one, two and three—one left, two centre, three right. The handler, if he is shooting, must be in the centre with the dog. Instruct them to approach the point quietly and without haste, aiming to be 10 yards to the side and about 1 yard in front of the dog, and to hold these positions as the dog roads forward.

A team soon learns to get into the best positions to cover the ground from which the birds are likely to flush, allowing for the wind direction and the slope of the ground. An example comes to mind of a moor which ended in a cliff falling to trees and grass below. Here birds always turned back over the guns, who needed to stay back and spread out wider than usual.

Birds frequently dive down a steep slope; therefore the uphill gun needs to be more forward and the downhill gun wider and more behind than on the level. Ask them not to shoot directly over the dog's head, especially if the birds have got up wild before the guns have reached the dog. Sometimes more birds are claimed than have actually been shot, as two guns shoot the same bird. The handler does not mind this, what he dislikes is no birds shot! Try to suggest that it is a long day and that everyone will have had enough walking by teatime. In this form of shooting everyone has to think himself into position rather than preserve the exact discipline of driving or walking up.

SHOOTING DIFFICULTIES

Shooting, I mean the actual firing, over the dogs has several problems. Good driven shots are often very

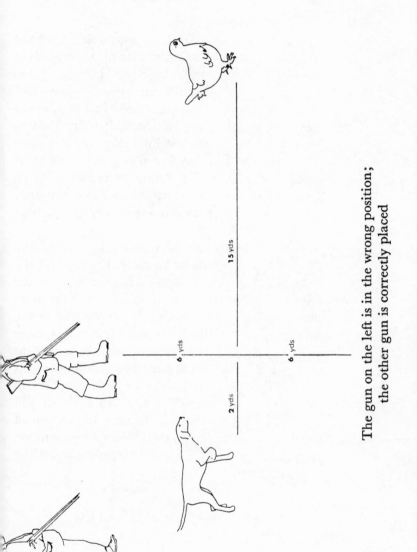

15 yds

6½ yds

6½ yds

2 yds

The gun on the left is in the wrong position;
the other gun is correctly placed

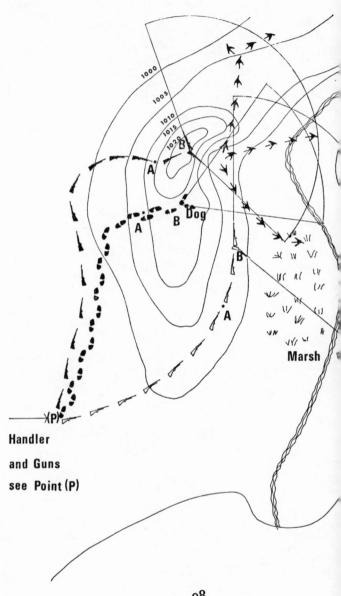

B
A

B Dog
A

B

A

Marsh

(P)

Handler
and Guns
see Point (P)

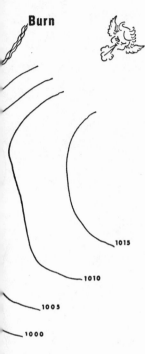

Burn

1015

1010

1005

1000

990

The handler and guns see the point at P. They separate to reach position A. All the men are still concealed by the contours of the little knoll. They then proceed to point B when the birds flush.

The right-hand gun can shoot any way they fly and has been concealed until the last moment.

The left-hand gun is concealed until near point B. He can shoot down two lines of flight.

The handler was concealed at A, but immediately comes into view of the birds. His arc of fire is limited on the left by the knoll and the right by the right-hand gun.

If all three had kept close to the handler none could have shot left. The right-hand gun kept under cover on the good going. The handler must get near the dog.

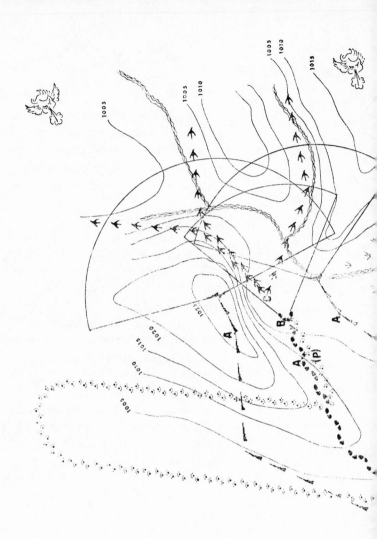

The guns, all walking together, see the point at P. They walk to positions A. The dog roads to B where the birds flush and the guns' arcs of fire are shown. The birds at C scatter. Birds going left are quickly hidden by the rising ground from handler and right-hand gun, but not from left-hand gun who is above them. Going right, all three can shoot, but right-hand gun has the best chance. All approaches made have used the rising ground for concealment. If all guns had gone to position P their chances would be much less.

disappointed in their performance. I put this down to several factors. First distractions: they watch the dog and not the area in front from which the birds will spring. They are distracted by the dog and the fear of shooting him. In their surprise, they pick the wrong birds, shoot too soon or too late.

Secondly, they may be standing all wrong, unbalanced by the rough or steep ground or unsighted by the contours behind which the grouse dip. The way round all this is to keep level or just in front of the pointing dog—wide enough out to shoot past him (as shown on page 97).

Study and plan the walk up with regard to the footing and the contours. Take the outside birds on your side. The plans on pages 98-101 may help to show what I mean.

CHAPTER 10

Dogging at Home and Abroad

Once the birds are pairing in the spring, training can start for puppies and field trials. In fact, only in May and June are the dogs unable to be used at all. I am, of course, talking of the amateur handler with the luck to have a job which allows him a few hours free in suitable surroundings each week. For the owner-handler, trials mean that his dog can be used almost all through the year—in spring trials, summer trials and the shooting season.

FIELD TRIALS

Field trials are very helpful in several ways. For the pointing dogs, conditions exactly reproduce those of the shooting day. A dog is asked to go out and find, be steady and get the birds to fly. His job is then over. No birds need to be shot, though a shot is fired to test for gun-shyness. Damage to the birds and the future shooting prospects are minimal. This enables the hosts to hold the trials year after year without sacrificing their shooting and they are very generous about having them. Handlers and spectators accept that it is a great privilege to use the ground and take care not to cause damage or trouble.

A second great advantage of field trials is the incentive to train puppies for trials in the spring and July. It does not so much matter if they run or not, provided the handler is stimulated into going training. Trials are also a show piece for good dogs and a training ground for handlers. Stakes are varied to suit all tastes. They are truly open and all entries are accepted in accordance with the rules of the schedule.

Lastly, trials provide a good opportunity to see dogs which might be suitable mates for your bitches if you are thinking of breeding.

CONDITIONS ON THE CONTINENT

In Britain, the game laws make the game the property of the land-owner; they define game and limit the season when it may be taken. These laws are accepted and supported by the public, and as a consequence game is plentiful and driving the easiest way of harvesting it. Abroad, the position is different; game seems generally much more scarce and driving unsatisfactory. Dogging is the most rewarding method and pointing dogs are far more commonly used. Because almost all game is shot over the point, the pointing dogs can be, and are, used to retrieve it. They are invariably able to mark the game, and

blind retrieves are not common. If they point a fresh
live bird, it only adds to the excitement and the bag.
In Britain, retrieving is thought of in the context of
drives, blind retrieves and the need to hunt through
the scent of live birds. Specialised retrievers are
therefore much more satisfactory. Retrieving by
pointing dogs can make for unsteadiness, with the
dogs slipping off and pointing instead of searching
for the dead. Really keen pointing dogs do not seem
very interested in dead birds.

In France and Belgium conditions are similar to
England and at field trials game is plentiful. Com-
petitors are numerous and are only tried once in the
stake. This puts an emphasis on style, on point and
speed. The dog is run for a definite period then re-
turned to the car and a dramatic point remembered.
The dogs are beautifully trained and do the job very
well. The French and Italian public professional
handlers, with their assistants, seem to train great
numbers of dogs in a season.

In Italy they have partridge and quail. The quail
sit very tight and the dogs working for them go very
wide and fast. In field trials which I attended, the
grey partridges, quail and hares were plentiful. The
occasional pheasant was not counted in the competition.

In the Alpine areas, woodcock are also a favourite
quarry. In Scandinavia both the game and the
conditions are very similar, and English dogs adapt
themselves readily. The basic training and qualities
of the dogs are the same everywhere, but it is

necessary to retrain dogs for unfamiliar conditions.

THE AMERICAN SCENE

In the USA, field trials and shooting over dogs are very popular. Guns, judges and spectators are usually mounted. The dogs hunt in a much taller cover than is customary in Britain. The elevation of the horseman is necessary to see down into the cover. Having a mounted handler allows the dogs the utmost freedom in hunting. The trials that I have seen in America were most exciting and the greatest fun, with everyone cantering about the country and charging to see the point.

REQUIREMENTS FOR DOGGING

Clothes and footwear

A very great deal of one's time dogging and training seems to be spent in a cold wind. A light, waterproof wind-cheater coat is therefore essential; this can be opened, turned back, carried in a bag or strapped over the shoulder when too hot, is wonderfully warm in the wind and keeps one dry. If rather too large, it keeps one's bottom dry. I favour 'plus twos' for the legs, with thick stockings. They dry quickly after showers and seem less tiring to wear. Waterproof trousers can become very hot and heavy during a long day. In any event it is not really 'on' to continue dogging in a downpour.

Gum boots and various other types of rubber boots are popular. I do not like them on rocky going, and heather tends to get into them. Leather boots or nailed shoes seem to me the most sure-footed and comfortable, even though one does get wet feet. Some very hardy souls wear tennis shoes—I should hate to do so when carrying a gun.

Dog transport

Dog transport is always a problem. A Land Rover is probably ideal, as I think dogs travel better without too much view around and are much less prone to sickness if mainly enclosed. For this reason vans with solid sides are better than station waggons. I cannot bear the idea of putting dogs in the 'boot' at the back where they are both invisible and inaudible to the driver.

Guns and cartridges

You may be inclined to go for a very light, small-bore gun, but I think the temptation to fire long shots makes this rather cruel, unless you habitually shoot with, say, a 20-bore. I am certain that a cartridge belt is the best way of transporting cartridges on a hard walking day. A belt is also helpful to the handler, if he is shooting, as a dog anchor.

Lunch

On a shooting day, you may be asked to take your lunch with you. Remember that beer is very heavy to carry and burn water a pretty harmless substitute.

Epilogue

Speculating about the future can be fascinating. Can a guess be made as to the prospects for the pointing dogs?

THE PAST

The capture of game for the table dates back a long way in Britain and was more important in early days than it is now. William I's game laws were more concerned with the larder and less with sport. A daily diet of bacon, salt beef and salt fish must have greatly enhanced the pleasure derived from roast partridge!

Since the earliest use of pointing dogs for netting game, three lines of technical advance have been changing the picture. In farming, better ploughs and larger draught animals enabled more land to be brought under cultivation, as well as opening up the countryside. Improvements in harvesting machinery

—from the scythe and sickle to the reaper and binder—changed the stubble and pastures.

The muzzle-loading shotgun, at first too cumbersome to use for flying shots, took the place of the net. The improved muzzle-loader and increased farming produced conditions ideal for the pointing dogs—open country, plenty of weedy stubble, a slow rate of fire. This was probably the time of their greatest popularity.

But changing farming methods reduced the weeds and stubble, and breech-loaders increased the rate of fire. Preserving and rearing pheasants became the great thing. Shooting ceased to be an informal meeting between two or three friends going out in the dog cart for an hour or two. It grew more organised and social, and involved walking up or driving with six or seven guns. Shooting was more of an early autumn occupation; people shot in September and October, and used their horses to go for a bump round with the hounds from November onwards.

Bags became bigger and driving more expert. The super game shoots developed, with their loaders and two or even three guns. The talk was not so much of how 'Ponto' held the covey in the roots as of the size of the bags. It became competitive and great shots travelled by train from end to end of the country to boost their host's bag. Dogging was in eclipse and not socially acceptable. This change had not occurred in 1848, when General Hutchinson first wrote, but was well established in 1880.

New factors began to alter the picture once more. Income tax and death duties hit the big estates, and huge preserves became more difficult to finance. The shooting syndicate was the final outcome, with even more intense game rearing. Unfortunately for pheasant driving, the more birds reared the harder they are to show properly. If too tame they do not fly, if too wild they just are not there!

Meanwhile the use of chemical sprays and powders as weed-killers and fertilisers greatly harmed the insect population, both by damaging the insects themselves and killing the vegetation on which they fed. Increasing population led to loss of farm land and, in combination, to a great fall in partridges and some other birds.

THE PRESENT

Today, partridge driving is becoming a rarity and the bags have recently diminished dramatically. Driving with too few birds becomes a very chilly and dull occupation, but the dogging enthusiast does not need or expect too many birds. The interest is not chiefly in the number of slain. He is on the move, warm, and absorbed in the movement and charm of his dogs. He is constantly scheming to try and outwit his quarry. His fieldcraft is most important.

The super game shot stands at his peg during the drive, pots the birds like the snooker player from all angles and at all distances. If they do not come his way, he can do nothing about it. He does not scheme or place himself; his host does all that, and to be safe he must be disciplined.

The man shooting over pointing dogs can be discriminating, only shooting at cock pheasants, or leaving the large coveys with their young birds for the future and concentrating on small lots or barren pairs. His guest is also much more involved in that he must use some skill in placing himself and forecast the flight of birds. Both still have the joy of a good shot and the misery of a bad miss.

Unless urbanisation spreads to such an extent that you are more likely to see a lion behind a fence than a wren—quite a possible development in the South of England—the dogs can give fun over areas in which driving is not feasible. Dogs can also be used where partridges are too few for driving but sufficient to give a little sport before the pheasant shoot starts.

THE FUTURE

The numbers of pointers and setters and of their owners have increased more than four times since 1947, and the opportunities of using them seem also to be increasing; but the dogs must reach a certain standard to benefit by this trend. If they are unsteady to point, they are in the way of shooting; if they do not beat the ground properly, they miss too many birds and have too many accidental flushes. They must also, however perfectly drilled, have some natural ability so that they can show bird-finding brains. In the other types of gundog work, faults are not quite so obviously damaging to sport, although some manage to do quite enough.

Pointers and setters are not easy to hire without the handler, because careless handling can ruin them—either by spoiling their drill or, much worse, by overworking the best dog until he is exhausted and damaged in style and health. I have seen first-class dogs so damaged in ten days that they never really recovered their health and well-being. The keeper who handles hired dogs simply wants birds killed and will do nothing to bring on the others—very frequently he does not know how.

In my opinion the opportunities are available to anyone who can produce a team of reasonable pointing dogs and spare the time to handle them. Because of the very high cost involved, a big driving day necessitates that the ground is suitable for a very high game population. Much ground, which is unsuitable for the bigger numbers of birds for driving, will produce a fair show for the dogs.

Index

Page references in italics indicate plates or diagrams